# HAPPYNESS IN YOU

# HAPPYNESS IN YOU

A Poetric Journey Within
A Mind In Love

KENAN ALMASRI

| Library of Congress Control Number: | | 2020908511 |
|---|---|---|
| ISBN: | Hardcover | 978-1-9845-7840-2 |
| | Softcover | 978-1-9845-7839-6 |
| | eBook | 978-1-9845-7838-9 |

Print information available on the last page.

Rev. date: 05/08/2020

**To order additional copies of this book, contact:**
Xlibris
1-888-795-4274
www.Xlibris.com
Orders@Xlibris.com
810097

# DEDICATED TO MY EVERYTHING

Never Stop Being You

*Love is a reality laying distilled behind our own ignorance or acceptance of its very existence or departure. A blinding force of nature meant to drive action within those who have the strength to unleash all that their hearts withhold amongst another while lacking the expectations of a requited response. For it is the mere effort that leaves us fulfilled as any regret or anxious thoughts slowly departure. It is all we are.*

# CHAPTER 1: WHEN I FIRST...

# WHEN I FIRST LAID EYES ON YOU...

*Her hair had curls that ravelled the imagination and graced the eyes as they began to seduce your sense with the aroma they held within them. A mountain of silk cushioned for the cheek of the simple individual who could easily drift off with their face within it. A smell that unmistakably captured the scent of a garden as it allowed your mind to release. To release and lay victim to the thoughts that liberated the beauty it was surrounded by and merely be drifted away into an unconscious consciousness. A bed of hair that leaped from the canvas of divinity. As if she were a creation held within time to capture all her beauty. A painting nonetheless because one could not comprehend the natural existence that laid before them. Brush strokes of imperfect perfection.*

## WHEN I FIRST SAW YOU DANCE...

*She had a smile that was paralyzing but birthed a gratitude as one could find comfort in the feeling of an incapability of movement. To be frozen in time for the mere sake of losing yourself in that smile. It was as if nothing else mattered or held any material value over the warmth that caressed your body whole. An inimitable feeling that your heart was in safe hands and a reassuring oscillation that vibrated from her very presence. A smile that was of its own stature and perspired the fragile touch of beauty that it had been so gently graced with. It was a state of happiness that was contagious in the manner of reminding whoever was fortunate enough that happiness was no longer a pursuit. Happiness was not for another day nor for another hour. Happiness was simply in that moment. Happiness was simply her.*

# WHEN I FIRST FELT YOUR SOUL...

*Purpose. It is the single requirement left in the hands of
each individual birthed into the fleshing existence of Earth.
It stands sufficient amongst us as if to reassure the common
man of every step he takes. Purpose was in her for every
step she took was one that furnished the concrete floor that
seemed to openly cushion itself as if her feet were to be graced
by pillows rather than the stiffness of its nature. Every smile
she cracked tethered deeply into the souls of its victims as it
unleashed its celestial character upon them. Almost as if it
sheltered a striking resemblance to the heavens that found
home in between two gently soft cheeks that held firmly on
her face. Every hand she shook was left melted in the essence
of the softness that laid its prints, almost as if her skin was
immersed in silk. Everywhere she looked was embellished by
beauty and left needing more. Almost as if time itself had
needed to slow down to simply digest the nature of her gaze.
Eyes that glowed a dark brown but held within them the
purity of a soul that shined in its broken upbringing. Eyes
that were almost healing in a sense of their innocence taking
nothing away from the wrath they were capable of.*

## WHEN I FIRST LONGED FOR YOU...

*The waves crashed upon the shore with a thunderous roar as if they were to battle the rocks that bordered them. Burnt photos laid gently at the deeply birthed ground of the water as if they awaited resurrection from their perpetrators. The moonlight shined ever so bright as it glistened across the mirror like water that complimented it with a sparkling welcome. The mind sat there lost and out of place attempting to find peace and solitude in the natural beauty that was orchestrated before it. It looked up into the stars in desperation as if to align the dots in attempt to map out life. To no longer attain the feeling of misplacement in a world where one can be grossly astray. Perhaps answers did not lay clear but it was peace that seemed to calm the aggravated mind that juggled its many questions. Rain began to fall ever so graciously as if to hug the cold skin and comfort it with a familiar feeling. Love. An idea spat out in existence but simply missing. Maybe that was no longer the case.*

*Sophisticated but beautiful. Complex yet intriguing. It was the mind of a woman that had been challenged by the world and the inconsistencies of life itself. A mind paralleled by nothing except that of the mazes of the ancient Greeks. A labyrinth one must enter and pursue with the utmost care and attention to detail for it all to even begin making the slightest bit of sense. But it was her and the curious individual could ask for nothing more. It was a transparency that was nothing similar to the clarity of thought that satisfied the simple mind but one that reflected the true divergence of her. A uniqueness that shined in a refreshing glow like that of the sun shimmering on the calm waters of a beautiful river or a pond out in the midst. One drawing attention yet one just out of reach. To tread with care and attention. A guideline for what was to come and what could be. A reinforcement of the bold yet nothing short of true statement that she was not to be assessed at face value. A depth that captured the heart and stimulated the mind. A depth that consumed itself within the questions you could not help but ask. A reminder of the beautiful sum of a cruel world. The mesmerizing art of a struggle that one could only be grateful for even beginning to understand.*

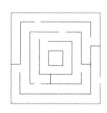

## WHEN I FIRST WANTED TO KISS YOU...

*Never in my life had I seen a light shine so bright as if to make a man forget about the common misconceptions and complexities of life. Yet it stood shining through her as if that was her sole purpose without her knowledge making it all the more mesmerizing to the soul. For an individual to be unable to comprehend the energy she emitted in its lifting power. Simple yet disillusioned. It was a blessing in life that one could not question for its vast propensity to provide answers would never be enough in the gaping hole of our intuition and curiosity. It was simply meant to be enjoyed. She was simply joy.*

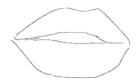

## WHEN I FIRST TOLD YOU I LOVE YOU...

*To reach over and mend the pain with the gentle touch of her palm and fingers that had found themselves wrapping and tightening around mine. It felt natural. Almost as if I had existed in a life of sin for the mere fact of foregoing such a simple yet logical feeling that was feared for its ability to be lost in translation. What had existed in those moments was a nurturing of the mind that would in return feel a contagious warmth and inexplicable glow that destroyed all thoughts, leaving nothing but bliss. It was almost as though no thoughts needed to exist in such moments for all that they were can be embodied in that of distractions. Unnecessary inconsistencies taking away from the big picture. She was inevitably and undeniably nothing less than the big picture. It would be a mistake to label such divinity as an escape from reality in light of its capability to root your soul to the Earth and remind you of just how comforting the sun could be. To remind you of how beautiful moonlight can be in the absence of that comfort. To remind you of the gentle breeze coated with saltwater alongside the rocky shores you don't visit enough. Her existence was not an escape but a reminder of an angel's true capacity to shine through the purity of the human heart.*

# WHEN I FIRST LOST TRACK OF TIME WITH YOU...

*Time didn't exist around the presence of the glistening beauty that had blessed my vision with its appearance. Nor did any rational thoughts or calculations. There were no stirring ideas nor doubts nor worries. There was just her. To live in the very second that life had to offer was a fairytale before she had graced my existence. It all seemed like a fairytale but at the same time couldn't be because of how grounded she had made me feel. How important she had made me feel. How vulnerable yet secure she made me feel. A happy ending wrapped with a ribbon on top.*

# WHEN I FIRST STARED INTO YOUR EYES...

*All I could feel and hear was the calm presence of the wind that playfully struck my hair and face in an attempt to relinquish my thoughts of the crushing anxiety they felt. An anxious reluctance to accept what was before me under the dim starlight that would attempt to reassure my eyes of the actuality of its existence. For what was the point of living in denial and choosing only to search for the downfall in circumstances. To pluck every flaw in an attempt to lift a barrier between yourself and the common adversary that was life. The moon sharing a comforting glance as it emitted its ominous glow to reaffirm my judgement as I took one final gaze. Beautiful. Inside and out. For beauty was man's greatest weakness especially that of the soul. I never thought my heart would skip a beat ever again. I never thought my eyes would find their addiction. I never thought my hands would find their everlasting warmth.*

## WHEN I FIRST SAW YOU SLEEPING...

*Never have I had a moment where the very breath that laid dormant in my chest had escaped in the smoothest fashion. A long exhale followed by a comforting warmth within my soul as my eyes peered over to witness the angel that laid next to me. I looked around to remind myself I was not elevated within the fantasy and figments of my own imagination but that I was truly living. A succulent display that had filled my eyes with ecstasy in its artistic and mesmerizing nature. I felt frozen for the very fact that I never wanted to look at anything else again. Calm breaths left her nose as she embodied all that was peaceful underneath eyelashes that gently shuttered as her mind run free. Hair that seemed as if it was ready to grab you within its never-ending curls and refuse to let go. You yourself accepting such a predicament because you never want it to. Hands that were cupped together as innocent fingers intertwined one another almost calling your name to grab ahold of them. Lips that laid gently shut with a brush of pink suitable to every part of her that screamed and uttered an unmatchable flawlessness. She was an anodyne. She was my anodyne.*

## WHEN I FIRST OPENED UP TO YOU...

*Lost in a sea of tears I wondered in despair of the eluding question that simmered in my ears and the very innards of my mind screaming, "Why is life so cruel". Drowning within the lucid liquid dripping from cheek to cheek I glanced towards the grim grey sky for answers as if it would reach with a helping hand and a quick response. Instead there you were. Perhaps you were all the response I ever needed standing in your cool demeanour across from me. A smile that was contagious stretching from ear to ear with a slight interruption at a dimple that accented your purity and beauty. The cuts on my arms never seemed to phase you nor my propensity to lose myself within the darkness of my mind. You stood tall and proud, accepting the clutter that made me who I was.*

# CHAPTER 2: THE WAY YOU...

THE WAY YOU RUN YOUR FINGERS THROUGH
MY HAIR...

*The manner in which the epitome of despair and
hopelessness was lifted off of my shoulders and chest so
swiftly, allowing me to release the pent up breath that was
imprisoned within me, was unprecedented. I melted within
your palms falling apart between fingers that gently collected
the pieces that shattered as you unconsciously reassured
my mind that they were safe. Pieces that were not to be
reconstructed in a form of your choosing, but ones that
were accepted for what they were. Damaged as can be and
spat on by the society that long was considered home to the
fragility of the heart that made them. Palms and fingers that
simply became the necessary cushion to relieve the stress
that had wound up and tightened around me. A cushion of
unfathomable beauty and unparalleled understanding. An
acceptance of me.*

## THE WAY YOU COMFORT ME...

*The pure-hearted are a rare and scarce commodity that an individual would be lucky beyond measure to acquire. To hold and even begin to call theirs. But there you were. Allowing me to feel accepted with pockets as shallow as can be but a heart that was full nonetheless. A mind that was satisfied beyond its wildest dreams afloat in a world where things just began to make sense. A moment of clarity was amidst for your capability to challenge the clutter that dragged my thoughts into the dark. Your presence was enough among few to none to provide solace in a place where it seemed nonexistent. In a place that seemed to be worth no ones time to even try nor believe in. A place that was frail and held up only by the mere bandages and tape that strategically placed themselves to hide the damage. Yet around you the damage was visible, hiding behind nothing, but causing no pain. It was merely accepted. Accepted by an angel with a heart of pure gold and warmth that swept you off your feet and held you in grace, passion and love outweighed by nothing other than the simple innocence that shined through her eyes. Precious.*

## THE WAY YOU SMILE AT ME...

*In the promptest manner there it was, ready to capture my soul and thaw the ice around the long forgotten icebox within my chest. Ready to proclaim and reiterate the very thought that it was for me. A smile that seemed so undeserved for its mass propensity to emit a purity that was unmatched by the simplicity of its counterpart. However, it remained nonetheless as would the flowers that sustained the stormy rain or the leaves that fought the urge to freeze within the cruelty of winter. To be swept off my feet by a split second action in light of the innocence that graced my eyes was inexplicable. Perfection never existed till that very moment where I began to realize that such an idea of mesmerizing sublimity began and ended with only her. I felt as if I could have stared forever only in continuous conversation and question within my mind if my eyes were deceitful. Scared to glance away for a split second in worry that such a dream would collapse in an instance or fade as would the snowflake that melted within your palm as soon as you held it and called it yours. In admiration and awe my body felt still and my mind in the mass chaos of thoughts had found solace. I never knew I was surrounded by darkness till I was bedecked by such light.*

# THE WAY YOU MAKE MY STOMACH FLUTTER...

*There was always a subtle inability to explain the vibration that overcame you around her. It was almost as if your soul had left the vessel that imprisoned it in order to witness the innocence it had felt. For seeing was believing and a feeling that outweighed all else had to be questioned for an inability to understand its existence in the first place prominently hung over your head. A glance that had made you feel like you were the only thing that mattered. That you were important above all else and that your presence was valued. An ideology that dumbfounded the darkness that crept up on you at the spur of the lonely nights. Your mind rattled with questions and confusion as if a storm was brewing in beginning to accept the nonfiction account of life that was unfolding. Only to have a calmness swept over it as the sun overtook the harsh and malicious appearance of the clouds and rain through her simple touch. Clueless of her impact and unmistakably unaware of her grace had she sat there only to give you the time of day you yourself did not feel you deserved. A product of celestial nature that you could never begin to earn, but one that you were grateful for in every passing second.*

# THE WAY YOU LAUGH...

*The sun could never begin to replace the perception of warmth that overcame me in the company of the music my ears had the fortunate pleasure of vibrating along to. Nothing could compare to the aroma and energy that was the pinnacle of what true happiness had felt like. What true joy had looked like. An amazing sight outweighing its surroundings or what had now seemed like the illusion of a cruel reality. A facade the common man had agreed to be the generally accepted understanding of what existing meant. A false reality that had shattered with her mere laughter like glass in representation of the frailness and instability of such a lie. She was living proof that jubilation was more than a possibility but a product of living. A laugh that outweighed the obscurity of the dim-lighted thinking of our thoughts and one that made you believe. Just as the rainbow arrives in rescue of our sight after the astringent rainfall, it was a laugh that could rescue you every single day.*

## THE WAY YOU TREAT OTHERS...

*A touch of compassion. A sprinkle of empathy. A dash of inspiration. A cup of kindness. Two table spoons of understanding... To watch a woman go about her day with the recipe for "Being Extraordinary" in the utmost flawless and smoothest fashion is an addiction for the eyes. Eyes and a mind that cannot be able to apprehend the organic nature of an angelic presence unaware of its capacity to effect and influence the life of others. To propel them forward with an unconditional guarantee of reassurance and a shoulder to lean on. An extraordinarily beautiful soul compacted into a gift and offered to those that have the fortunate pleasure of experiencing such a woman in their life. Offered in no form of transaction but in the construct of immediate charity to all those that may or may not need it. It made sense. For what is the purpose of "being" when one lacks an effect on others that drives them forward. An act of purity set forth with no intentions as it stands to represent nothing more than the character of an angel. An angel I have fallen in love with.*

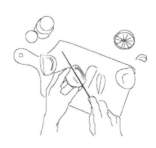

# THE WAY YOU HUG ME...

*To be held in the arms of gracefulness and assurance was a feeling out-rivalled by none in its ability to drown you in an aroma of safety and vulnerability. To finally let go and unravel yourself, handing your heart whole to her in trust of the caring hands that ensured its safe being. And in doing so slowly melting onto skin glazed of a silk caramel that you now have found to be home. A gentleness matching the liking of a soothing voice that giggled as you drifted away into dream land. For reality had not presented a possibility such as this. Yet there it was. Cupped between perfectly comforting palms that had felt like the world to you. That had felt like your world. In its mass sensibility and prospects it shrunk down to a goddess that could fit around your waist. One you hoped would never let go of you.*

## THE WAY YOU LIGHT UP THE ROOM...

*To grab and hold two cheeks that encompassed the very breath that had given you life was beauty beyond measure. Perfect skin of a tan complexion sitting calmly within your palms that almost shook from the nervousness that accompanied the pleasure of witnessing something so pure and fragile. Your heart began to be overwhelmed with warmth and sat beating comfortably. Loneliness was no longer a misfortune and dread had escaped your thoughts as you slowly lost yourself in eyes that wholeheartedly gave themselves to yours. A magnitude of connection incomparable to the magnificence of supernovas. It was silent and intangible yet it was existentially there. The sole ability to feel vulnerable and weak to your knees, ready to let yourself go in an exposition of everything you had to offer. In a composure drowning of certainty and dressed in emotional solitude, you sat wondering if she could ever understand. If she could ever understand how much her voice had brought you peace or her gaze had brought you tranquility and a sense of importance. How her touch had left you wanting more or how her smell had brought you an escape from the cruel thoughts that suffocated your mind. Lost in her only to remind yourself that in this moment of complacency, you were finally found.*

# THE WAY YOU LISTEN...

*Being human is a pleasure lost in context within its altered definition in a crippled society of expectations. It is the state of transparency and acceptance of oneself never made easier around an individual like her. To finally have a shoulder to lean on in times of need capable of standing tall and still in its glory. Like mountains impotent of movement regardless of the powerful wisps of the wind that challenged their position. Strong but gentle, it was allowing you to finally feel understood or merely heard with compassion and empathy resonating beyond the comforting singing of birds or the still calmness of moonlight. Ears that opened to your voice like the gates of heaven, giving an undivided attention in reassuring you that within those mere seconds your worries were acknowledged. Hands that held yours in the beginning of a consoling tenderness. A human in their natural state of response to a clustered mind in need of rescue. A gem, kind enough to share her light when yours just ceased to shine bright enough. A treasure, that enriched you without realization of the wealth it possessed or even began to share. Yet there you were, a man of riches in account of her presence, and once again, a man that felt human.*

CHAPTER 3: DATE #...

DATE #1...

*There was an overwhelming feeling of anxiety that overcame every trembling bone in my body in a sane response to the unfolding events that had become foreign in nature to me. My palms began to perspire heavily in parallel reaction to a shaky voice that rang in tune with the hesitant creaks of an unsteady wooden door. My heart pulsed heavily, beating on the innards of a chest that with each knock, came closer to being torn wide open. And then she spoke. A cool gentle wind waltzed across my moist forehead and reminded me why I was there in the first place. There was something different about her; a familiar statement that never seemed to echo so loudly before in certainty. A rigid and trampled interaction seemed to slowly manifest into a smoothly flowing and nothing but natural connection. Calm as snowfall or as inherently senseful as the tide overstepping onto the sand off a beach. "Have we met before?", A voice spoke in my head out of mere confusion for the soul it had connected with so purely and deeply. "Maybe not in this life".*

DATE #2...

*I could sense an unearthly addiction forming. One that crept its way into my life unexpectedly and began to consume me in the mildest manner. The urge to see her smile or merely hear her voice had become undeniable in its strength and tenacity. It was as if every single thought was intercepted by the idea of her, almost to say that in these moments, nothing else mattered. The feeling of a dull existence began to escape me almost as poison being drained from its victim. The mirror seized to be my mortal enemy in the few seconds that my mind had only digested thoughts of her. Lost in my own eyes that hid behind a channel of glass, I was finally able to find love for my parallel counterpart. To had met someone who accepted whatever pieces of me were left, ignited belief within my soul. A light that grew dim each day had burst into flames in what I hoped would be a finale to its tragic history. A belief in life and a belief in myself.*

DATE #3...

*There was an innate sense of a lack of control over the insecurities and realities of my life as I consciously chose to let go of the large drape that covered them whole. The magic trick that held in front of all others seemed to be profusely unnecessary around her. My heart had leaped at every opportunity to reel her closer to the life I had called mine in an effort to truly feel known by another human. Time was but a number and carried little importance in the degree to which it would begin dictating the right course of events. Clocks had fell and shattered from their place in the unassuming chimes that had called upon to me to reconsider the rationality of things. My response was that of little amusement as I swayed confidently in the opposite direction. My mother was my rock and my soul and there was nothing more that made sense than an unveiling of that to an individual so special and refined in their nature. This is me.*

DATE #4...


*Laughter was a familiar sound around you that grew louder and more welcome with each visit. It found its home in your presence and unleashed a redolence of warmth and repose. To feel loose from society's strings and shackles that dragged you around as the puppet most accepted to be, was difficult beyond measure. Yet there you were, without a single care in the world and disconnected from any expectations effortlessly. A shocking sight to witness yet one that reassured me that in that moment I would rather be no where else than with you. Laughter that led to dancing and indescribable joy as we were surrounded by nothing but average people. I swivelled my head and realized I was the luckiest man in the world. I held in between my hands, the waist of a woman that was anything but average and that feared nothing except the uneven rhythm my feet displayed in a sorry effort to dance the night away. Yet there she was doing the same and unknowingly immersing my thoughts with bliss. They no longer were calculated nor doused with reason. They just were. And there was nothing else I wanted them to be.*

DATE #5...

*I love you.*

DATE #6...

*Watching her naturally light up the room as soon as she stepped into it was a sight that words could never begin to describe. It was as if she was naturally able to belong in any setting, never truly rooted in a comfort zone that was distraught from the immediate reality. The individual could find themselves simply immobile in the trancelike state her presence could leave them in. She had this profound ability to make things seem so simple in a contrasting ideology to the social anxiety the common human would feel but choose to mask. Joy. She emitted an abundance of joy that was infectious to everyone around her. Joy that would reach out to you with a long arm to wrap you whole and sweep you off your feet to carry you away to her reality. An invitation that was open-ended to all and selfless in its capacity to allow you to feel free. A freedom that came from the lack of judgement that would so often taint your demeanour and envelop your organic thoughts. A freedom that arose from an unfiltered and most pure version of you.*

DATE #7...

*I have never been one for change when it came to the small consistent aspects of life that seemed to just consume you in their comfort. Yet there I was sitting across from you staring at a plate of inane atrocity for the simple fact that you had inspired me to, and rightly so. Glancing from my serving and across to you I was at a mental crossroads in deciding what had looked more appealing to my eye. I felt as if I could stare at you forever in trying to piece together that the work of art a meter in front of me was physically real. Lost in a place where no thoughts wondered freely for they had been long evicted, I found a steady calmness identical to the one that came across you every morning at 5AM. The few seconds your eyes would battle to stay shut only to find they were wide open in conforming to the tranquility of singing birds and early sunshine. You became my 5AM and you could never understand it. An idiotic look on my face accompanied by a similarly ridiculous smile pressing up against each cheek was inevitable, only to have you catch me in my trance with a question of "what?". In the hollowness of my mind there was no answer but the single idea that you were my 5AM.*

DATE #8...

*There is always a persistent feeling that mirrors the rummaging of butterflies within my stomach when I am around you. Ones that fluttered in their beauty and grace in failed attempts to escape the fine barriers of my gut. I stared at you relentlessly almost in blank expression as I lost my words or the ability to speak at the sight of your lips. Luscious lips of faded pink that looked as soft as the clouds on the sunniest day. Neon lights had surrounded us as they brought even larger attention to the smile that appeared on my face automatically. I made every excuse to wrap my body around yours in trembling fear of making the foreseeable move of grabbing your cheek and sinfully leaning in without knowledge of whether or not you would do the same. I restrained myself, perhaps due to a lack of courage, or for the mere excuse I had made of ensuring you were ready for that part of me before it was offered so anxiously. I felt like a kid all over again.*

DATE #9...

*It felt as if we were immersed in the music around us that slowly began to dissipate and fade into a shallow sound in her presence. There was an inability to distinguish between the feeling of simply moving slower than everything around us or millions of light years faster, only to state the point that when I was with her, I was on another planet. Invited graciously by her, an entity not from this world, to join her in the intergalactic realm she had made home. A home where one lacked the necessity to question their purpose or life around them, for everything just made sense. She made sense. People came and went following the light that seemed to shine ever so brightly around her yet nothing seemed to interrupt the bubble I felt that wrapped me whole with her in it. The music began tuning in and out of focus as I lost myself in her carelessness and sheer joy, stopping only to occasionally awaken my body to do the same. There was an indescribable vibration that trickled off each hair on my skin when it came to music around her. It was as if I had been deaf and could finally hear. It was as if I would finally begin to feel true felicity.*

DATE #10...

*The diner doors seemed to be swinging open and shut
as nothing else could explain the jaw-numbing cold that was
overcoming us. I looked up from my blue fingers and across
from a laptop that within that second only seemed to spew
gibberish, to see you. Suddenly, the noise of the crying child
behind us or the cries of plates and forks waging war against
each other seemed to no longer exist within this vacuum of
time I lived in. It was the state of feeling okay. The pins and
needles picking at my brain that had been turning its gears
at speeds never before recorded had finally surrendered.
Another second more and I would not have been in shock
to see grey and white fumes escaping my ears. You grabbed
my hands that seemed to swallow yours whole and said,
"Hey silly.". I felt the numbness of my limbs as well as that
of my heart slowly deplete as I dissolved from an icy fortress
and made acquaintance to the saint that sat at my eye level.
As she smiled and looked away I moved my lips in gentle
whisper to speak not into existence the words, "Marry me..".*

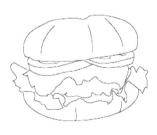

CHAPTER 4: BUT...

# AN INVITATION...

*The mind can be a citadel of pure darkness in a refusal to accept the concept of happiness and positive events. It is a pessimist at times. It is your worst critic. Welcome to my mind...*

# BUT I AM NOT ENOUGH...

*But there it was. This sadness that crept upon me like a shadow. A shadow in the sense that it was attached to me crawling closer and closer to my existence waiting to consume it whole. It was the predator and I was the prey. The incentive was any shred of a soul I had in which it was ready to devour whole. To swallow it in its vast dark desolation as it moved from one victim to another. It attached itself to my everyday life, waiting for any peak moment of happiness as its chance to rise and bring me down where I belonged. The pit of divine despair and agony filled with insecurities that would beat me down 15 feet into the ground. To the thoughts and destroyed desires that would haunt my existence each time an eyelid would close. An insomnia of suffering that left my chest aching with a pain. It was this indescribable pain that seemed to be a normal aspect of my life. To feel as though someone was reaching inside me with a closed fist trying to make it from one side of me to the other. To leave the hole in my chest that felt as though it existed all my life.*

## BUT I AM NOT NORMAL...

*Madness. It was something that I was accustom to, and far too familiar with. It was as if my veins imploded with the very idea of it. Peace was a dream I was never able to fully grasp nor find in the clutter of a life I called mine. No, instead it was madness. Madness not in the form of a chaotic life but madness as an idea of something that lived within me. A storm that raged with winds that could break bones and crashing waves that capsized ships whole. Madness. Just an inability to ever be able to piece together the thoughts and words that bounced off the corners of my brain violently. They rocked me back and forth and displaced me from the natural world. As though I belonged to another dimension, I never seemed to be completely nor closely in tune with the life around me. I walked each street corner and felt as though no one batted an eye at me, like I didn't matter. I believed that if I vanished off the face of the Earth no one would ask about me.*

# BUT I AM SCARED TO BE JUDGED...

*I have always believed that faith is a gift. That faith is not something you earn, nor a skill that can be crafted but a gift. It was a gift that I had not yet received. Faith was awarded to those who chose not to give up in a world that was so cruel and corrupt in each corner of life. To those that were able to stand tall in an existence that pushed them down, in a living that wasn't a living at all. A day to day life of standards and a society of judgements. Opinions and minds that screamed with disapproval witnessed across the eyes that gleamed in the shadows. Watching, in grudgeful patience behind the blinds of their artificial lives and false smiles. The handshakes that grasped you with the gold Rolexes that shook along with them only in ignorance of the fact that they'll be same hands to bury you. The same hands to stab you in the back with a cold blade that will shiver every bone in a fragilely unaware body.*

## BUT SOMETIMES I BREAK...

*I believe that the ability to forget is a blessing. The ability to move on from memories and a past that could haunt you was somewhat of a dream come true. To be able to live through life being able to pretend that darkness never existed, that pain was never suffered, that delirium wasn't experienced. An ideology I fear at times I am not accustom to. I am haunted by these memories, the ones that had torn me apart and left me feeling so alone in a world with so many around me. A feeling of emptiness in rooms filled with people. A lack of direction in a world filled with compasses and maps. I am victim to letting these memories dictate my life in moments of vulnerability. I let them entrap the person I aspire to be as they chew at the sparks of positivity that light up inside me until eventually there are none. I retreat within myself in a lonely chasm held together by a loneliness that ached. Secluded from the rest of a world that I wanted no part in. A world too cruel. A world too rugged.*

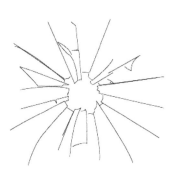

## BUT I AM LOST...

*The street lights illuminated a path for me along by the moon that was shunned each day by a selfish sun. Rain poured over the cold streets as it drenched me in its painful drops that fell ever so elegantly from the sky. There was something about the rain that I grew fond of. Perhaps it was its ability to mask the tears that fell from each cheek thunderously as I took each step forward. The tears that cried names and crimes. The tears that remembered the wrongs and the rights. Tears that felt cold to the touch of skin that simply grew old of the air it was surrounded by. The air of the wicked; circulated around those who committed the crimes, who witnessed the wrongs and stood by. Skin that felt as though it would melt in the shower of this acidic water pouring graciously from a dark origin. A sky that was a witness to all that was around it.*

BUT ALL I KNOW IS PAIN...

*Pain is an addiction. It is the ultimate search for life in a world where a soul can be so lost, so helpless. It is a cry for help. In an everlasting womb of agony surrounded and entrenched by numbness, we search for any significance in our living to indicate we are still here. Pain. Maybe it is the epiphany that the individual man has been calling upon in explanation of his each breath. To bring context to the reasons he stands tall each day and pursues fictitious dreams. Dreams that are so easily collapsed. So easily bought. Dreams that are birthed in mere minutes, parallel to their death quick seconds after the fact. Each gasp for air a desperate question of "what is next?" or "why?" whereas the returned response holds few to no answers. The human turns to pain. An infliction of wounds that seems to propel past the abyss that consumes existence whole. A feeling of livelihood that encompasses some purpose living within it. Drops of blood to add definition to a life so dull and lost of colour. The loss of purpose. The loss of incentive. The beginning of nothingness.*

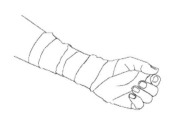

## BUT MY MIND IS DISORDERED...

*I was a man neither imprisoned to the thick walls of iniquitous nature nor equal to the higher being that freed himself from them. I was a man stuck in the middle fighting no circumstances other than those of the mind, the hardest battles of them all. My mind was one of cruel upbringing with the simple intentions of displaying a hatred amongst its host, myself. It was equivalent to the clouds that selfishly steal the light at any opportunity available. To rain knives violently down on the flowery thoughts that had started to flourish as if their purpose was to die before ever living. It was a storm that crackled harshly at the sailor attempting to find safe passage, revolving around him to encompass a situation that offered no escape or nowhere to turn but to accept the fact of living within anarchy. Living only to die.*

*Emptiness. It was a familiar feeling that lacked the necessary definition in order to be confronted in the appropriate manner. It laid dormant waiting for the opportunity to engross the light that was inevitable in a life of balance between beauty and darkness. A worthy adversary in a lone conversation or debate in its purpose to convince the individual of their worthlessness and isolation. It was a debate that was more often lost on the side of humanity that endlessly forgets the roaring inspiration of the people in life. People who were meant to serve the single purpose of supplementing the lives of each other and harnessing the energy required by not only themselves, but by others. It was as simple as the clouds that had rained not only to release the weight that had built up within them, but to feed the grass, the flowers and the trees that sat patiently waiting for the mere moment of liquid divine intervention. It was only then that the vegetation would acquire the gratefulness for its friends above, as it quickly forgets their existence when they are not around, making the unconsciously conscious choice of falling back into the abyss of seclusion. Emptiness.*

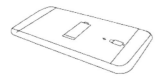

# CHAPTER 5: AND THEN YOU...

## AND THEN YOU SAID HELLO...

*It was a greeting but so much more than any ordinary hello. It was one of those hello's that reassured you in its eccentric confidence and unmatched sincerity. A hello that held you incapacitated in your very spot from the lack of familiarity to such a higher form of nature. A hello that swept you off the ground and carried you away into an enchanted sanctuary guarded by the beautiful specimen that initiated such a reception. You had me at hello. You spoke and I saw nothing but the mere butterflies, birds, and rainbows that appeared around you as if I had been intoxicated by your very presence. Held to a state of mind far from sobriety but one that nonetheless you never wanted to escape for its organic composition. Your voice travelled like music as it vibrated within every ear that had the fortuitous luxury of being graced by such a sound. My memory never fails me in recalling my immediate response. One that held a voice shakily and a posture of a nervous wreck. Hello.*

# AND THEN YOU GAVE ME YOUR TIME...

*Time is a concept floating within our universal existence brought to reality by the very entities that inhabited its planets. It became a necessity. A commodity. It was as if conversation no longer held value for its ability to satisfy the emotional and mental craving of connection but stood to only be an asset if a price tag was attached. That ideology slowly seemed to drift away as I dove deeper and deeper in dialogue with you. Stunned at the fact that a girl like you gave a man like me the time of day and an unwavering mindfulness, I felt a breath of fresh air attack the skin that laid lonely on my face as if to give it a reminder that such a comfort existed in life. That such sincerity was rare but was attainable nonetheless. You listened to me pour my heart unto your open ears and palms for hours never lowering your gaze or looking the other way. Instead you delved into the hazel pupils of my soul to listen only to understand. A notion I had felt I was foreign to. For as long as I can remember, that was the first time I truly felt important.*

## AND THEN YOU ACCEPTED MY MIND...

*Acceptance was a form of love and comfort that I had never been accustom to for my inability to ever recognize its existence within my life. It was the unfamiliar feeling of being understood for no other reason other than the fact that an individual had cared. The capability of stepping out of your reality to temporarily but earnestly enter someone else's was one that spoke magnitudes to the heart and character you possessed. This was a scarce feeling and an action undertaken by close to none, but not with her. She seemed to be able to comprehend all my worries, problems, and demons as if they were her own. She had this innate ability to enter my mind, no matter how hard I struggled to voice my thoughts. She always found her way in. To finally feel okay in an existence where "okay" was a forgotten state of living and one that seemed so far from possible as my mind had been ripped from the tethers of reality. She sewed it back together. She brought sanity to the madness. Peace to the anarchy.*

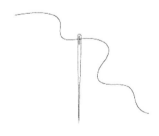

## AND THEN YOU WIPED MY TEARS...

*Tear drops rolled off my rugged skin as they crashed thunderously with the bat of each eyelash that had shrugged them off unwilling to harbour their arrival. They found their home in the uneven concrete as my shaking had evicted them from the comfort of my face. There were perhaps many reasons for the birth of these liquid knives that pierced my soul with their existence and sometimes there was no reason at all. Yet it was a memory that shattered the cruel darkness of this living with all its light and glory that inspired its animation with two palms and a finger as adorable as an infant's. One that reached across this sea of tears and had began to wipe their origin every so gently. Two eyes that had crossed gaze with mine and lips that mouthed the words "don't cry" as I struggled to recall an answer. She was a reminder of why those tears no longer needed to exist. Why the agony I felt was no longer welcome. For each time I had glared at those eyes and lost myself in their reflection of my soul I was once again loved, comforted, understood.*

# AND THEN YOU MADE THE PAIN DISAPPEAR...

*To wake up in the morning without the presence of a crushing weight on my shoulders that day after day seemed to make my back atrophy whole, was a dream. It was an unrealistic state of mind that came ever so quickly with the thought of her. The single idea that seemed to leach off my mind as a parasite and find home in its prey began to dissipate. It was the thought of a lack of belonging or importance. It was a chasm that stretched longer than the Nile and was equally as slippery to be in. Slippery for both its conniving words and your ability to lose your footing in it. But in a trance that was revered for a sudden ability to walk on water it seemed as if the chasm was powerless. It no longer held me imprisoned to its dark escapades that would envelop the reality I strived for, the happiness I longed for. She was the trance that made it all seem possible. A vision of ecstasy that overcame you with a delightfully overwhelming sense of acceptance and purpose.*

# AND THEN YOU SHOWED ME YOUR WORLD...

*It was an anomaly to be introduced into another individual's life. Not in the form of fiction charades or the masks that society had become accustom to inhabiting. But a warm welcome into the transparency that more often lied behind closed doors in a reveal of trust and honesty. Trust and honesty that were delivered to you with a lack of payment or requirement of a returned asset. It was merely an instinctive reaction upon simple interaction. A woman that was capable of not only the ability to understand, but the selfless action of offering her soul to those that crossed her path on a daily basis. An offering that came to any and all for the mere reason that it was her subliminal belief that life otherwise was in a lackluster of defeated purpose. I was a lucky man that crossed her path.*

# AND THEN YOU KEPT ME GROUNDED...

*I was not immune to the sudden victimless feeling that arose as a sudden disconnect with life so frequently occurred. The complex circumstance of the mind that seemed to elevate you past a formal experience with the world around you. I was lost. Adrift from the ideals that I preached were of the utmost importance to life and misplaced from the elementary pleasure of living. Anxiety attacked the weak walls I had built to defend a mind I shamefully called my own as the brittle fabric of its nature would collapse without a fight in embarrassment. This was a battle that raged within me every second I was ungrateful for the beat of a heart that sluggishly kept me alive. That is, until I met her. I could never wrap my mind around the fact that her company seemed to not only melt away the pressing worries that entangled my mind, but it altogether brought me back to Earth. A voice that seemed to instructively allow for my return to the positivity I so adored but struggled time and time again to upkeep. She was a blessing. Perhaps it was my love for her that ignited the forceful need to reorient my mentality, or perhaps it was just the idea that an individual could be so perfect. Perhaps it didn't matter. She was a blessing.*

## AND THEN YOU INSPIRED ME...

*The mediocre and effortless task of arising among the screech of alarms that never seemed to cease became ever so gruelling. The act of simply starting my day became questionably arduous and unlawfully difficult. It no longer made sense for the lack of reason that instilled itself in our rising wake. This was the pervasive case that haunted the endeavour I called life until she overcame my thoughts. My mind was filled with nothing except notions of love and the drive to be the better individual that a woman like her deserved. The mornings became so much more than a welcoming of the sun and a calmly departure of the still night, but a moment of admonition that screamed "you matter". That the woman that encased the ideas flying within my mind was a beacon of prospect. A beacon not out of reach but one so close it threatened to blind you with its light. One that infiltrated the darkness in its angelic composition and inspired you. This is the mere beginning of a thank you.*

## AND THEN YOU SAID "I LOVE YOU"...

*I yelled and screamed at the top of my lungs because nothing was able to contain the excitement and sheer life-satisfaction I experienced. The world seemed as if it had desisted from its rotational responsibilities and everyone around me was no longer present. It was me, the moon, and the thought of her in the account of the words she had spoken so gently into my ears. The gaping hole in my chest no longer ached as I metaphorically gazed down in surprise of its sudden structural repair. I felt complete. It is possibly the most challenging task to attempt to deconstruct the perception of completion but it is undoubtedly an unsurpassable state of mind. The roads never seemed emptier as the lights took physically impossible shape, dismantling in the essence of time that no longer was my reality. I love you.*

# AND THEN YOU SAID YOU WERE MINE...

*There was a requirement of each passing second to pinch myself in friendly reminder that the life I was living echoed in reality and not a false universe I had concocted. That she was real and an individual with a heart of gold was truly a possibility in this life. That I was a man that was spoiled with the fortune of her. In her simplistic ideals and manner of life I had come across a needle in a hay stack. A woman with the utmost purity that came across and devoured the insecurities you held so close to you. One that seemed to shine a promising glow in confrontation of a sun that could not be more grateful to provide its illumination to a work of art like her. It had seemed to be as if the birds chirped louder around her along with the grass and trees that grew greener. A life that had encountered a complete shift in lens from a cold portrayal to one of warmth. She was warmth. She was growth. She was everything.*

CHAPTER 6: DD/MM...

07/12...

*In the lack of confidence that overwhelmed my wellbeing from time to time, I had always possessed a love for the ability to converse with another. When I had seen her across the room my heart had sunk in my chest, displaced from its origin or correct situation. I lived by a law that seemed to govern my life ever so scarcely, only being called upon during moments of the utmost need. I believed that anything that overwhelmed you with fear could be combatted within 10 seconds of your time. I walked across the room until I had made eye contact with her. My breathing had levelled its pace with that of an olympic swimmer as I maintained my composure with the 7 seconds I had remaining. Reaching her and opening my mouth to not only ensure I had her attention but that the conversion would not cease to exist after that moment was a gruelling 5 seconds of my time. In the 2 seconds I had left, I met her pupils that seemed to be dazed in the confusion of the aberration of the events unfolding. My skin perspired ocean waves of evidence that this was not a regularity for me. With a grin on her face and eyebrows that maintained a cool poise I asked for her number knowing I would not be victim to letting what I felt diminish with the simplicity of a short dialogue. The 10 seconds had ran their course as a sigh of relief and a smile on my face embodied the conclusive feeling I felt. "Goodbye" was now "see you later".*

56

14/12...

*I had almost forgotten the pleasure of courting a woman in an attempt to expose your heart and begin to learn about hers. It was an event that gathered dust in my mind for the calamities that time had brought unto it. It no longer existed and was tucked away underneath the thoughts and concepts that echoed louder in their relevance to my life. Yet for the first time in years I was to call upon it. I was undertaken by the ghastly breaths my lungs reached for. It was as if I had forgotten to breath with her by my side and unconsciousness was soon to be knocking on my door. The tunnel vision focus on my breathing was interrupted as soon as she spoke. She had the power to make things seem so simple. The walls and nerve wrecking thoughts that surrounded my mind seemed to collapse with each sentence she delivered. I was reminded that my memory would not aid me here. That she was special. Instead, I began to admire and she did the same.*

01/01...

*I was never one for the excitement that came for so many in light of the introduction of 365 more days. For some it was a rebirth and an affirmation that change was a possibility. For me, it was but a continuation of all the heartache that life had to offer. The challenges and interruptions that seemed to engulf any stride one would take to move forward, only to send you three steps back. Yet I remember seeing her on that god-forsaken day. Suddenly I was like everyone else. I believed. It is my conviction that faith is a gift and I cannot begin to explain the faith in life that surmounted me that night in her presence. She was the gift I had longed for. The gift that everyone needs.*

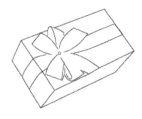

12/01...

I remember looking across the miniature table that seemed to barely house my large arms and cozily comfort yours. Looking at you as your hair reached long past your shoulders to twirl in ways no science could ever be able to record. Lips that seemed to glimmer under the poor lighting and eyes that regardless of that fact still seemed to harbour a shine that was inexplicable. I ached to reach over and grab you in confession of all that I felt. To scream to you that you were perfect in every manner possible. That you were a woman of sanctified possibilities. I wanted to voice the reminder that wherever you walked heads would turn in awe. The magnificence you embodied was unmatched by any other human that took physical form and tried to compete with you in my eyes. But I knew that doing so would risk insanity. I looked at you and calmly commented on how beautiful you were as my heart shattered into pieces from all that it felt and yet the collectedness it was expected to maintain. Little did I understand about how you felt. All I knew was that I wanted to call you mine.

27/01...

*The touch of your lips on mine could only be described as a cool gentleness equivalent to a chilled cloud recovering from the outskirts of a rainy day. It was heaven wrapped in a blanket made of silk and tied in a golden ribbon made into the shape of a bow. It was everything you had hoped for and more than your dreams could ever fathom. You were left with this feeling of mild dissatisfaction because you simply could not get enough. It felt like the beginning of an addiction that you were simply to accept because every shed of willpower that found home in you had no objection. It was perfection. You wanted to grab her with hands that wrapped her cheek and gently slid onto the cusp of her neck. Your grip slowly tightening because every fragment of your being did not want to let go. A foreign feeling. A thing of beauty. A touch of peace.*

23/02...

*The lights and the music meant nothing without your company. They would have been almost obsolete if not for the 5'6" dose of silky smooth skin that was curved as if cut with the finest edges and sanded down to perfection. She stood in your presence moving in perfect harmony with the sounds that seemed to be in superlative pitch and coordination to her every shift in dynamism. You placed your hands on hips that were welcoming of your gentle touch. Gentle for the sole reason that you were afraid of the fragility of such excellence. All the people around you and her seemed to slowly fade out of the picture as you were left with her eyes and lips that you could not take your gaze off of. The feeling of the music pounded in your chest in a reaffirmation of living or was it merely the feeling of immense love and complacency you felt? You knew it didn't matter for all you wanted to do was put her body alongside yours and move in conformity. It was beyond her comprehension that she had the ability to elevate any experience she had the pleasure of partaking in. "Dance with me forever" you murmured in silence that was defeated by the loud sounds that crushed anything you had to say. She looked at you and smiled. You needed nothing more.*

22/03...

*It was the beginning of a new chapter for me and I didn't even realize it. It was something that left me tossing and turning for days in a pursuit to acknowledge its being as I pinched myself in an attempt to convince my mind that it was facing reality. And for the first time in a long time, that reality was a blessing. I held her, something that I could never begin to quite understand. I made excuses as if to dedicate my lack of comprehension to delicacy or a uniqueness in life that was frightful in its scarcity. But the truth was more visible than trees making home in vegetation. It was the simple fact that I felt undeserving. It was an ingrained belief within my soul that the world was geared for adversity and that when such antagonism was no where to be found, I was ready for it, expecting nothing more. The truth is, you are happiness. A concept I have long forgotten for its lack of consistency. You are mine and I'd like nothing more than to remember it. To redefine it. With you.*

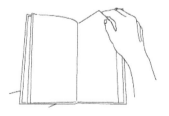

# CHAPTER 7: WHEN I GAVE YOU...

# WHEN I GAVE YOU A "GET WELL" PACKAGE...

*In comparison to lifetimes, I had only known you for the equivalent of seconds. But that seemed to be as insignificant as dust rolling on the sidewalk in effective reaction to the wind from the bolting cars and kicking feet. It just held no value in my eyes as I looked for any excuse to make an impression on you. I felt overwhelmed by this sudden urge to care for you in a time of limited need for anything a man like me had to offer. Yet I was driven and compelled. It was as if my heart had already been sold on the idea of you. Sold for the reason that it could not get enough of you. My mind rambled with excuses to see you and to offer you my version of love. It had long been damaged and criticized by no other than myself but that no longer mattered. I wanted to be with you.*

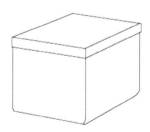

# WHEN I GAVE YOU ROSES...

*You looked at me in a storm of confusion as if you had never seen flowers before in your life. You lacked any understanding for why an individual like myself would take the time and think of you. It was as if you had no idea what you deserved as you turned your head and looked at me for what I perceived to be ages before you uttered the word "why". I had no rational reason except for the fact that they were beautiful and so are you. You went on to profess that your mind had only associated such offerings with circumstances of regret and apology. That you were only worth a man's time when he had left you in tears or discomfort. That flowers were an eraser that was meant to take a page that had been distorted with the shambling of poor action and hurtful words, and make it new. My heart broke to pieces that day as I analyzed the seriousness of that statement that escaped your lips. I looked at you with pupils that dilated immensely as if wanting to reach out themselves and hold you to say, "you deserve flowers just because...".*

## WHEN I GAVE YOU CHOCOLATE...

*Nuts covered in a shell of dark brown that screamed "I am yours and I am here". Chocolate had long been a slice of heaven that delivered itself to you unapologetically from a silver platter of divinity. It was a short fuse of time where your taste buds had elevated past the pain you had felt kidnapping your imprisoned mind with them. It was the first time I witnessed you in discomfort. It was as if your mind had dissociated from your body in a way to escape what you had just felt. I looked at you, barely knowing you, and my eyes felt the liquid pressure of a tear that wanted to burst from its oval cage. I had no right to grab you and say "its okay". I had no place to hug you and ask what was wrong. Instead there was an instinctive retreat to the uncomplicated option of chocolate. Circular homes to comfort that I could not offer you myself. A medium to connect my heart to one that was displaced from happiness.*

## WHEN I GAVE YOU A RING...

*Love will always have an innate ability to make any individual lose all bearings of common sense. The intelligence to sit down and process the right decision or the right course of action becomes a moot point. Action overwhelms thought as your psyche is shut down along with the conscious voices that dictate your decisions and evaluate the consequences of planned undertakings. I could make the excuse that all the shimmer and glory of diamonds and jewels had been irrefutably irresistible as I made my way past the store. That necklaces, rings, and bracelets had escaped their ever so clear glass cages to chase me down and escort me into their trap. This would make everything easier to explain. To justify. Yet the truth echoes in the very fact that I saw someone so pure yet seemingly unspoiled. Neither with love or the materialistic fibre of objects. I saw someone suitable for a crown that no one had offered. This was my offering. A mere beginning.*

*The mind is a beautiful thing. It is a map with many twists and turns that in most cases causes the familiar feeling of being lost. It is a place of tricks and smoking mirrors that elude you and place you far away from the roots of your ambitions at times. It is a storage of absurdity that wanders in different shapes and sizes and forms. The mind is a storm raging from city to city with whirling winds picking up homes and vegetation only to chuck them out miles from where they belong. But the mind is sometimes your only escape, your solace. She had this mind that left me in awe. It was not a storm nor a map with an inconclusive ending. It just was. It coexisted with the life she was physically present in, never objecting to her thoughts nor causing havoc in the form of insecurity. Her mind was her Amber Room. Her mind was her eighth wonder of the world and it deserved a voice.*

# WHEN I GAVE YOU A CRYSTAL...

*Alexandrite was a crystal I had long held on my person for my ridiculous belief of its power to finally bring me in touch with the universe I had felt so disconnected with. It was an object I carried with me in an attempt to foster faith and a belief in better things to come. I never spoke to its magnitude or the meaning that it held within the vulnerable foundations of my life. All I knew was I no longer required it. It was you that I had found faith through. It seems counterintuitive to state that I felt a deeper connection with myself in use of you as the medium, but it was nothing short of the truth. I felt in tune with the man I aspired to be regardless of the missing path I needed or my method of execution. There was vision. There was clarity. Giving you what seemed like a meaningless relic at the time was one of many thank you's and a marking of a milestone for myself. It meant everything.*

# WHEN I GAVE YOU THE LETTER...

*I find a fond memory in how many papers I had crumbled in an irrefutable rage and frustration that arose from finding the right words to confess to you how I felt. The pen never quite seemed to flow miraculously on the paper as I had hoped it would. Instead it came alive in all its whitty remarks and criticisms in light of the words I had chosen. I had never argued with a pen before. But this was a first. A mere cylinder of ink my enemy, along with a tall, white, and blank paper that was our battlefield. How do you begin to confess every single emotion you felt on paper when your tongue struggled to voice these perceptions in the first place. It was a mystery. Nerves had found their final straw as my mind began to collapse on itself. It was only when I had shut it all off and let my heart speak did it begin to make sense. In a defiance of science and globally accepted notions, the mind was not a place for emotions. Instead it was a place of questioning which I had become tired of. To let these questions go and forget about what is sensible was what was required. It was an offering of me. All of me.*

# WHEN I GAVE YOU A MEMORY BOX...

*It was the beginning of an "us" that to my slow realization you needed affirmation of. To the uneducated individual it was a box of garbage yet to me it was everything. A collection of objects that in and of themselves represented the memories I had with you in the short time I was graced with your presence and company. Each object had spoke multitudes with a lack of words but an ability to spark light within me. It was timeless and it meant the world. Here is my world...*

# CHAPTER 8: I WISH I...

# A CONFESSION...

*This part of my heart was meant to voice regrets. The little actions and hesitations that in a glance at the past you wish you could change. I realize however, regret has no place in my heart. Here is my exception...*

# I WISH I WASN'T SCARED...

*A storm brews inside me as I try to conquer the barrier that lifts itself in strength and tenacity to defy me from my origin. It stands to be resisting me from all that I want to be or offer. Fear. It manifests itself within me as it finds company beside the hardships of a past that seem to arise in memory during the worst of times. A fear that history will repeat itself or a fear that digs its roots in my inability to accept the dim lighted parts of my existence. The fear that I am lacking what you deserve. It holds me in confinement within a prison of my own mind. Unable to escape this abyss of hatred I lose myself. I am no longer there. I look in your eyes for what appears to be ages only to find a reminder that you are worth the fight. The internal struggle. A reminder to strive to be nothing less than what my heart defines me to be.*

CHAPTER 9: YOU ARE...

## YOU ARE BEAUTIFUL...

*My eyes had widened in disbelief, unable to shift their gaze on anything or anyone else. It would have been almost insane to do so. I was unable to move nor pivot away for I was locked in a trance. I always believed beauty was a subjective concept that fiercely shifts with the eye of the beholder. This was the exception. It was a display of perfection that in the simple act of witnessing its essence did so much more for you than you were willing to believe or realize. A smile that lit a fire within your heart and a laugh that echoed across your physical presence. Lost in what seemed to be vibrations within water for the slow movement that everything around you had encompassed. Nothing else mattered as you let yourself go in eyes that sparkled right back at yours in assertion of the response you had to her existence. Your imagination imploded only to rebuild itself to include the idea that such a sight was possible. it was a redefinition of beauty.*

# YOU ARE SIMPLE...

*It was a reality that was tough to accept for my disbelief in its ability to prevail through an individual's life. The act of being simple. Not in the sense that your mind was lacking the necessary sophistication to attract an individual through arousing the fundamental intrigue that love so desperately requires. No, it was a simplicity found in your requirement of those around you. A simplicity that echoed in the small fact that you needed nothing but their presence and their ability to emit goodness in this world. That was all. There was no search for the materialistic ideals or the constant confirmation of love one would expect from their loving equivalent. In your eyes, it was all translated through the ability to be present and to show the purity the heart holds. You required nothing more to accept the individual or love them powerfully. I was shaken from your belief that nothing else was necessary. In you was a shining beacon of true innocence and purity. A simplicity that ensured you were nothing less than a miracle.*

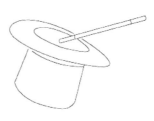

## YOU ARE KIND...

*The belief that life is driven by nothing short of the people within it was one I found lonesome in upholding. It was a conviction that every individual has a need for people and in response to such owes their purity to the world. Selflessness. It is an action that takes you away from all that you need and shifts your lens on a picture much bigger than yourself. It is living not only for yourself, but for everyone around you. It seemed as if she was never afraid to give up all that she had whether in time or prospect, to care after someone who needed such things even more. She had this inherent capability to step out of the shell each individual found comfort in, in order to give her soul to another human being. It was as if she was drawn to it without her direct realization of the fact. It was no longer a lonesome belief. It was one driven directly through her.*

# YOU ARE EXTRAORDINARY...

*The term extraordinary has been used loosely and tossed lightly at those that supersede the slightest expectations placed upon them. It was lost in translation for the longest time in my eyes as if embodying a piece to a puzzle that never quite fit, so it was placed wherever was deemed appropriate. That is, until I got to know her. An individual who encompassed the attributes to an extraordinary mind simply because of their drive in life and their attitude to its ever changing twists and curves. Her mind was beautiful as it was not only pure but inspired the same purity in others unintentionally. She had this capacity to gracefully touch the lives of others as gentle as the smallest ripple in water only to be blind to how large such a ripple would soon grow to be. She was nothing close to ordinary for her uniqueness and the shortcoming of any individual to make her comparable to another. She was the "extra" that we had all searched our whole lives for.*

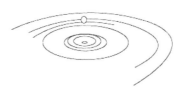

## YOU ARE UNDERSTANDING...

*It was an amazing sight to witness how easily anyone would be able to pour their thoughts and agony to her. There was a connection that she was able to form with all people that allowed them to untie the thoughts they had shamefully shackled to the deepest parts of their mind. A connection that inspired a sense of freedom within you. Your words began to flow unfiltered like water travelling in a steady and uninterrupted motion. You were overcome by this feeling that you were alone with her and she was the last person to judge you. A feeling that one would find greater comfort in than their own bathroom mirror. A feeling that the purpose behind such conversation was nothing less than the fact that your words were important and deserved an attentive ear to listen. A person that not only heard your cries but lifted themselves from their earthly vessel to place their soul within the conflicts of your life. An empathetic heart that stretched its abilities beyond measure. She was everything you needed and did not even know it. She was your saviour.*

# YOU ARE SILLY...

*She was always able to let go of everything that would hold the common individual back from being nothing but their true self. A choice to be as ridiculous and as unapologetically crazy as possible. I smiled so hard my face began to scream in agony begging me to stop. I just couldn't. It was an unmatched sight to share my company with someone who was just as unattached to what the world around them thought of their actions. It was a boldness that was infectious to even the most conserved victim. She was her own paradise that stretched nothing farther than the moment of time she was in.*

YOU ARE REAL...

*The world has given every human a multitude of reasons to form a barrier of protection between their organic form and the society amongst them. A reflex that has been cultivated through the calamities that showered painful knives of scrutiny in response to our attempt at living an unfiltered life. A life where we are true to ourselves and show nothing less. It is an honourable decision but one followed through by little to none. She had this bodacious dexterity to throw herself at the world with no regret or hesitation. As if the world's response never mattered in the first place or held no seeming value in her eyes. Her beliefs and actions as a person never seemed to falter nor shift as she unwaveringly revealed herself to society. To me.*

## YOU ARE HONEST...

*Her opinion was always readily available whether or not it was asked for. It was something that drove you crazy but you could not help but love it for its blamelessness. Lips that moved in direct coordination with a tongue that spoke unaltered by what was deemed acceptable or required by the individual fortunate enough to stand on the receiving end of such a conversation. It was honesty that came as swift as the switch of a lightbulb that burned brightly. It was everything you did not realize you required. Gorgeously smooth skin, wrapped around a mind that had locked society out. I could not begin to fathom nor understand the nature behind the intellectual pillars that held together the beauty before me. A beauty not in the sense of my attraction to her, rather an attraction to her candor. One that was incomparable and unique only to her.*

YOU ARE YOU...

*Never stop. Never change...*

CHAPTER 10: A DEDICATION...

# A REALITY...

*Love has evolved to become one of the most complicated concepts in life. It is surrounded by stigmas and infected with ideas of what is socially acceptable or sensible in the eyes of those courageous enough to partake in its endeavours. In the simplest sense, it has lost its definition. This is a dedication to true love, one lost in translation, and one misunderstood by many.*

# LOVE...

*Love is subjective. It is perceived by everyone differently and never seems to carry the same meaning to two different people co-existing on a planet we call home. No. It is never that simple in life. To some, it is their world. For every breath they take, life is given purpose and true meaning through the search for love and vindication of its very essence. It is everything. Life bleeds love. Life breaths love. This is a scarce population of individuals blinded by the journey to find reaffirmation in their existence through the power that love has to offer. A people that find faith in people. That need people. Unfortunately, it is never that easy. To wake up every morning and find joy through the offerings of not only your own travels but through the character of others is a dangerous choice. Some may find it humbling while others perceive this as suicidal ignorance. But, it just is. The mass of people will never be able to comprehend this lifestyle or manner of thinking as it is so far beyond their realm of living. They are a people that have made the conscious choice of electing the feeling of love as a mere product of life, accepting it in randomness rather than as a necessity. It is not purposeful nor powerful. Again, it just is. Yet, love is so much more than a reaction or state of being overwhelming your composure for mere seconds. Anyone unwilling or unable to understand its capability is instilled with the ideologies of fear. You may find yourself unraveling your brain and unwinding your mind in an effort to empathize with how love is barred through fear... It is the retched feeling or thought of not being enough. It consumes you whole. Swallows your inhibitions and the person you may have not realized that you are striving to be. The person you deserve to be. This stagnant thinking is derived from so many insecurities and a package of a past that your shoulders and back have been broken from carrying. It is not you. To live in a life filled with fear or a lack of acceptance of being able to truly love. To give yourself to someone whole with a lack of expectations to what their reaction would be, is miraculous. It is courage. It is purpose. The ability to let go of everyone who had harmed you. The people who lacked an appreciation for the absence of barriers or fictitious characters that you presented. The people who were simply not able to accept you. That is strength. That is faith. You must not live life in constant denial of your worth. You are worth magnitudes. Any individual lacking the ability to see what is right in front of them is living in denial due to their own fears. Their lack of acceptance of who they are. The only form of suicidal ignorance that is weary in the aroma of life is that people are not themselves. Every morning, individuals wake up with a choice that revolves around what mask to place over their true character. Why? Why are we afraid of vulnerability?*

# VULNERABILITY...

*Vulnerability means that you can be shattered. Broken. That feeling of your heart losing its footing and dropping to the bottom of your chest becomes real. The feeling of emptiness encompassed with disappointment that becomes unbearable is experienced beyond measure. For the average individual, this price is too high. It is irrational. I challenge that. Your ability to let yourself break over and over again only to pick up the pieces and let them redefine the origin of what makes you the human you strive to be is life, and love is not the exception. Your willingness to be fragile cannot be exclusive of what your heart desires. Love is the choice to let go. It is the release of all that you are. It is you. An offering of all the good and the bad gently placed at the reach of those you wish to accept it. It is the epitome of innocent honesty and should never be held to any standard lower than such. It is by that logic that society has dubbed such a powerful emotion as a fool's errand. An outrageous misinterpretation of vulnerability. However, it comes at a cost we must accept and conquer. It is a packaged choice of not only peace and beauty beyond measure, but internal turmoil. A place that will haunt you with its whispers of unworthiness and questions of misplaced thoughts. The price of unfiltered honesty is the expectation of judgement one perceives is a necessity of such action. Expectations kill...*

# EXPECTATIONS...

*Expectations are the root of all disappointment, pain, and agony. They are what cause the disconnect between our existence and the emotions we feel. It is why we have grown so numb, so distant from ourselves. It has become our choice to erase the possibility of emotion for the simple fact of the expectations that are paired with this endeavour. The expectations become too gruelling. They become unnecessary weight that haunts your every move across the various channels in life. You must ask yourself, in the rawest form of honesty, what role your expectations drive in your everyday life? The answer will never truly be concise enough to provide you with the solutions you are looking for. Expectations transcend our understanding but all in all are the ruins... They are the damaged buildings and torn down society's built within our minds of what could have been but just wasn't. What does it mean to have no expectations? Is it an approach to life that holds you accountable for nothing along with any of those that cross your path? No. It is the decision to let go of the weight that you have placed not only on yourself, but on others. It does not mean losing the essence of what you deserve nor the standards that you hold society to, but simply not letting yourself be eaten alive when such a society cannot uphold itself to what you adhere it to. It is the release of anxiety....*

ANXIETY...

*Anxiety is the flushing of your soul as it is dragged across the hypothetical mud and wasteland reserved in your mind for the toughest moments life has to offer. The most awful thoughts. It comes unannounced in levels that no one was prepared to battle. Each encounter with this contradiction of joy seems to differentiate from the last, both in intensity and timing. It is never the same and it is often in true transparency, a majorly relevant part of love. In granting someone access to your heart and the sophistications of your mind, it is almost inevitable to find yourself questioning it all. Glancing at the mirror horridly, lost in dumbfounded wonderment of yourself. Am I enough? What if...? Does he...? Did she...? It is a dark rabbit hole that is magnetic in its attraction for any state of mind. Whether it be true joy or the darkness that one often finds themselves within throughout the day. Anxiety will pour in through the small gaps of the wall of protection your positivity builds like water. It is a non-negotiable fact of life and an even more prominent event of love. It just is. How do we conquer it? How do we diminish not only our expectations, but the anxiety that is paired so perfectly with such a frame of mind? You must accept yourself...*

# ACCEPTANCE...

*Accepting yourself is a war that is waged daily without the necessary attention nor regard that the victim must reserve for it. It is a task that reads simply on paper but reveals its complications as one begins to face it. It is the marathon that your mind must partake in during the ultimate search for happiness. How can one begin to give all that they are, flaws and perfections, if they do not accept these attributes, if they do not love themselves first? It is a truth as clear as the sky on a sunny day emitting the reflections of the cool blue water underneath it. A truth that is clear but that is bitter in its taste and feel. Serving a heart on a silver platter to another person is already a noble task that takes courage, but doing so with a heart that you yourself do not believe in, is suicide. You must believe in all that you give, in every walk of life. The lack of confidence or acceptance for who you are and what you offer to this world will be the downfall of your ability to thrive. In accepting yourself, not only does it become easier to reveal every part of you, but it builds an understanding for what your happiness is....*

# HAPPINESS...

*The pursuit of happiness is the greatest unspoken dilemma that life has brought each individual to face since time had abruptly come into existence. It has been a grim search for many as each divergent experience has brought each human closer to their definition of what such an emotion is and how to manifest it. How to live it. The revelation of the fact that happiness is not a search, but merely a choice, will often come to very few. For some, it will take many trials and tribulations to discover this fact while for others, they have lived this reality since the day their lungs had welcomed the very air they require. Once you acquire the capacity to let go of the negativity that has been dwelling within you, and consuming you in the form of expectations, anxiety, and a lack of acceptance, you will experience joy. You will find yourself in a state of mind that has welcomed this experience without hesitation nor conditional requirements. Happiness lives in the very second you are in and asks nothing more than for your choice to accept its existence. It is not a chase nor a problem that requires the search for a solution. It exists within all of us, waiting to be empowered and unleashed for the rest of the world to see in its unique composition defined by only you. It is the question of whether or not you are willing to allow it. Live unapologetically. Love unapologetically.*

# A NOTION...

*Love is a notion I could never understand nor come to terms with due to its cruel nature, but it is alive nonetheless, afloat in the cool breeze that carries it across oceans and worlds altogether. It is something so powerful that it is beyond the comprehension of the individual's drive for survival in the abyss that swallowed it whole, called life. Perhaps love is the purpose in this dark, polluted reality, meant to drive us towards something larger than our simple being. A reason to wake up in the morning and smile, to chase greatness and simply stop running from the fears that sit mellow within us, but instead to face them with this newly found perception driven by love.*

THE END OF A BEGINNING.

*If love is crazy, then may I go insane. If it takes time, then may you have all the seconds I have on earth. If it takes my soul, then may you see my purpose. You are worth it all.*

I WILL ALWAYS LOVE...

Lightning Source UK Ltd.
Milton Keynes UK
UKHW010706240520
363742UK00004B/116/J